GEYSERS

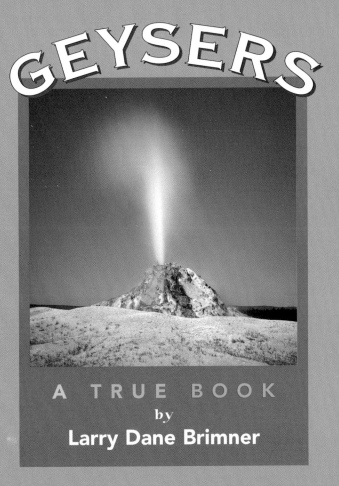

A TRUE BOOK

by

Larry Dane Brimner

Children's Press®
A Division of Grolier Publishing

New York London Hong Kong Sydney
Danbury, Connecticut

A geyser at
Yellowstone
National Park

Subject Consultant
Peter Goodwin
*Science Teacher, Kent School,
Kent, Connecticut*

Reading Consultant
Linda Cornwell
*Coordinator of School Quality
and Professional Improvement
Indiana State Teachers
Association*

Author's Dedication:
*For Sue and Dona and those
Freshwater Dolphins.*

Acknowledgment
*I am grateful to Sneed B.
Collard, III, for sharing his
scientific expertise.*

*The photographs on the cover
and title page show erupting
geysers at Yellowstone
National Park.*

**Visit Children's Press® on the
Internet at:**
http://publishing.grolier.com

Library of Congress Cataloging-in-Publication Data

Brimner, Larry Dane
    Geysers / by Larry Dane Brimner.
        p. cm. — (A True book)
    Includes bibliographical references (p.).
    Summary: Describes what geysers are, how they are formed, and
where they can be found.
    ISBN 0-516-20669-9 (lib.bdg.)   0-516-27190-3 (pbk.)
    1. Geysers—Juvenile literature. [1. Geysers.] I. Title. II. Series.
    GB1198.5 .B75 2000
    551.2'3—dc21   99-058038
                                                                          CIP
                                                                          AC

GROLIER
PUBLISHING

Contents

Old Faithful

Earth's Geyser Fields

A crowd of camera-toting people has gathered in the cool morning to capture a performance on film. Almost on schedule, a tall column of water and steam blasts skyward from somewhere deep inside the Earth. Cameras click. Once again, one of

Yellowstone National Park's most-photographed attractions, Old Faithful, has proven itself to be a crowd pleaser.

Old Faithful is a geyser, a natural spring that shoots hot water and steam high into the air from time to time. Hot springs are found in many different parts of the world, especially in places where there are, or were, volcanoes.

Hot springs form when water has seeped down deep

Geyser fields, such as this one in Iceland, include geysers and other kinds of hot springs.

Most known geysers are located in these five areas of the world. Yellowstone National Park, which spreads over parts of Wyoming, Idaho, and Montana, contains more than half of these geysers.

inside the Earth's crust where the rocks are hot. But not all hot springs become geysers. Conditions need to be just right for a geyser to form. In

Kamchatka, Russia, is the site of one of the world's main geyser fields.

fact, only about eight hundred geysers are known to exist worldwide. Nearly all the geysers we know about are clustered together in geyser fields in five main areas of the world.

Hot Rocks!

Scientists believe the Earth has four layers. We walk and play on the thinnest and coolest layer—the crust. Below the crust is a layer called the mantle. It is made of hot, liquid rock, called magma, that may reach temperatures of up to 7,500° Fahrenheit (4,149° Celsius). When magma rises into cracks, or faults, in the Earth's crust, it heats the water that creates hot springs and geysers.

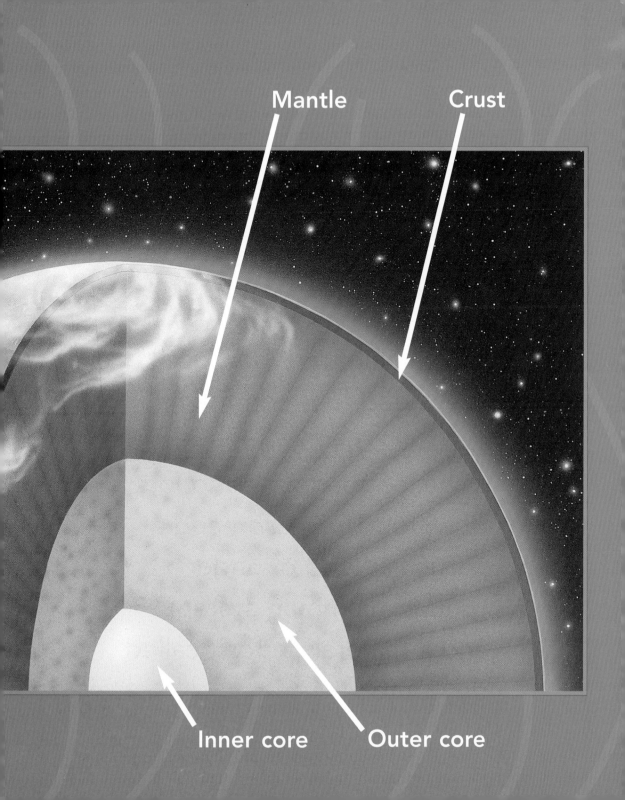

Mantle

Crust

Inner core

Outer core

How Do Geysers Form?

Geysers are rare because they need four conditions to exist. They need a source of heat—magma—and lots of water. They also need a particular kind of underground plumbing system and a mineral deposit called geyserite.

All hot springs have a heat
source and natural under-
ground channels, or plumbing,
that provide them with water.

A geyser's plumbing, however, has a special shape. At some point there is a narrow spot in the channel—usually near the surface.

The narrow tube causes water below it to be under great pressure and prevents the water from turning into steam at the usual boiling point. Instead, the water in a geyser's plumbing system becomes super-heated, sometimes reaching 500° F (260° C) or more before it finally boils and turns to steam.

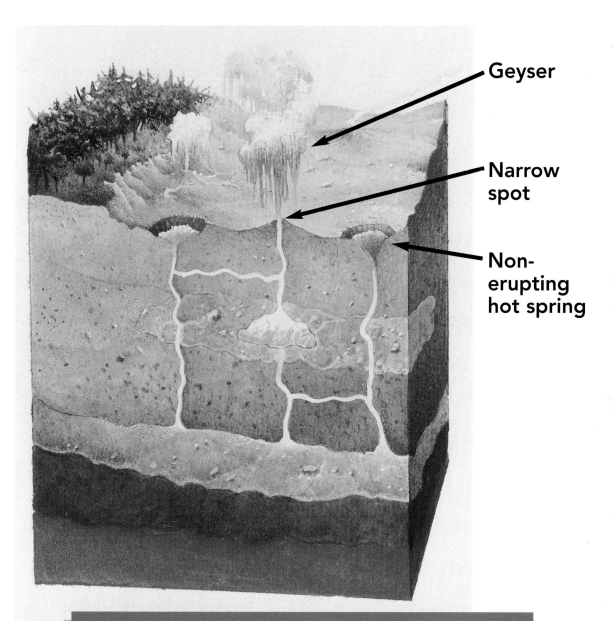

Geyser

Narrow spot

Non-erupting hot spring

Unlike other hot springs, geysers have narrow spots in their underground channels that put great pressure on the water below.

A geyser erupts because the water and steam in its plumbing system can't leak into surrounding rocks. Geyserite—a flaky, white material that forms when a mineral called silica dissolves in water—collects along the plumbing system and seals it.

But silica doesn't dissolve easily. So geysers exist only where underground rocks are rich in silica. This kind of rock is found in volcanic areas.

A geyser's plumbing tubes are lined with a flaky white substance called geyserite.

When these four conditions are met, geysers can form. But why do they spout? When the water inside the geyser finally

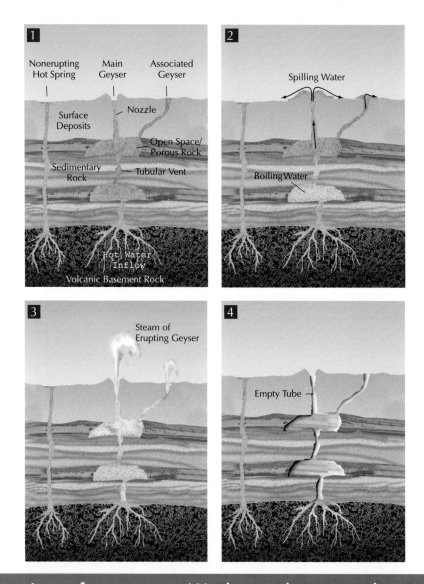

The eruption of a geyser: (1) the underground water is heated but does not boil because it is under too much pressure. (2) The water begins to boil, steam forces some water to spill out of the tube, and the pressure inside decreases. (3) The geyser erupts as more steam forces large amounts of water out of the tube. (4) After all the water has left the tube, the geyser stops spouting.

gets hot enough, it boils. Steam then rises up through the geyser's plumbing system. As it does, it pushes water above it through the narrow spot. Then more steam forms, and more and more water is pushed through the narrow spot. The geyser erupts.

When all the water has left the tube, the geyser stops erupting. Eventually, underground water sources refill the geyser's plumbing system, and the cycle begins again.

Strokkur Geyser, a regular geyser in Iceland, starting to erupt

Some geysers erupt on a predictable schedule, so they are said to be "regular." Old Faithful is a good example of a regular geyser—it erupts about every 76 minutes.

An irregular geyser at
Yellowstone National Park

Most geysers, however, are "irregular." Their eruptions cannot be predicted because their plumbing systems are shared by other hot springs.

Other Kinds of Hot Springs

A geyser field usually includes several other kinds of hot springs. These occur when there are only some of the essential conditions necessary to create a geyser.

A fumarole, or steam vent, for example, forms when there is very little water, but very

A hot pool in Iceland

A fumarole at Yellowstone
National Park

intense heat. By the time the hot water reaches the surface, it has turned to steam. A fumarole is the hottest of all hot springs. Steam blasts out of some fumaroles at temperatures as high as 284° F (140 °C).

When a fumarole lies beneath thick mud, it forms a mud pot. Steam from the vent sputters to the surface. Glubb! Blopp! A mud pot can sound and look like oatmeal

A mud pot (left) and a mud volcano (below)

simmering on a stove. If the mud is thick enough, globs of it may build up around the vent to make a cone-shaped mound, or mud volcano.

A hot pool occurs when there is an excess of water but not enough heat for a geyser to develop. Many hot pools are "painted" vivid colors. Yellowstone's Grand Prismatic Spring is one such colorful pool. Its colors come from the sun's light. We see blue when

sunlight hits air or water. We see green when it hits tiny plants in the water called

Yellow algae causes the yellow coloration around the edge of this hot pool.

algae or a mineral called sulfur. The yellow that we see around the pool comes from yellow algae.

Pink bacteria causes the pink coloration of Champagne Pool in New Zealand.

You can often tell how hot a pool is by the kind of algae or bacteria living in it. Bacteria are tiny, single-celled life forms. Many have adapted themselves to live and thrive at only certain temperatures.

Pink strands of bacteria, for example, like water temperatures above 180° F (82° C). Yellow algae like it a little cooler— between 155° and 164° F (68° and 73° C). Green algae grow where the water has cooled to about 122° F (50° C).

Geysers Under the Sea

In 1985, scientists were surprised to find geysers along the Mid-Atlantic Ridge. The Mid-Atlantic Ridge is a volcanic mountain range that runs along the ocean floor 2.5 miles (4 kilometers) below the surface of the Atlantic Ocean.

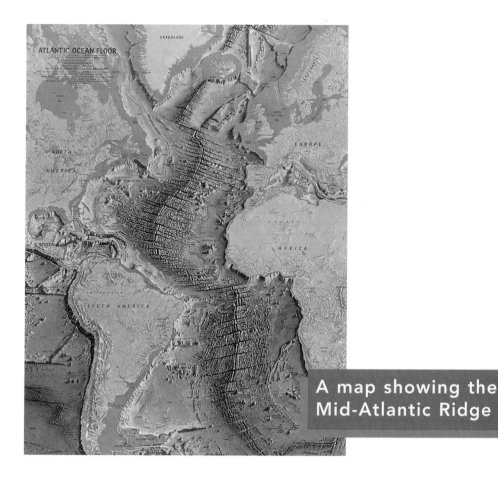

A map showing the Mid-Atlantic Ridge

Until this discovery, the only known undersea geysers were near the Galapagos Islands in the Pacific Ocean. These were discovered in 1977.

Oceanographers, scientists who study oceans, now believe that there are undersea geyser fields all over the world.

Hydrothermal, or underwater, vents exist wherever hot liquid rock escapes through cracks in the ocean floor. These cracks are caused when giant slabs of the Earth's crust, called plates, move apart. Cold seawater seeps into the cracks and becomes heated. Then it shoots upward, creating superheated steam geysers.

This steam carries with it
many kinds of minerals from
beneath the ocean floor. These
minerals build up around the
hydrothermal vents and sometimes form structures that look

like odd chimneys. Scientists call these structures black smokers. They belch black clouds of minerals—including copper, zinc, silver, tin, lead, sulfur, and gold—into the sea.

Undersea geyser fields are home to eyeless shrimp and giant tube worms—just two of the many odd creatures that have adapted to life in the hot, mineral-filled water.

In fact, these creatures could not live in any other

A black smoker near the Galapagos Islands (left) and giant tube worms growing at the top of a smoker (below)

environment. When nature destroys an undersea geyser field, it also destroys the strange creatures that live among it.

Black Smokers

Black smokers begin to form when hot, liquid minerals from beneath the seafloor turn solid in the cold ocean water. Black smokers form quickly—in a few months or years rather than in the millions and billions of years that geologic time is often measured.

The top of a solidified black smoker

Scientists report that one black smoker rose 23 feet (7 meters) in three years, and they can get even taller. Some reach 165 feet (50 m) in height when not disturbed.

Black smokers look like the chimneys you might find in a fantasy village. Sometimes they are shapeless clumps of orange, green, brown, or white rock, while others are towering spires. Many are topped with onion-shaped domes.

Geysers and people

Earth's natural heat is called geothermal energy. In some places, people have drilled wells that produce steam and hot water. These can be used to heat buildings and to make electricity.

But geothermal energy comes at a price. When wells

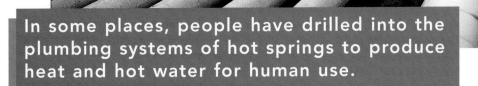

In some places, people have drilled into the plumbing systems of hot springs to produce heat and hot water for human use.

are drilled into a hot spring's plumbing system, they can damage geysers up to 25 miles (40 km) away.

Geysers change naturally, too. Geyserite builds up—at the rate of about 1/100-inch (1/4-millimeter) per year—and eventually chokes off the vents. Earthquakes rearrange underground plumbing systems, sometimes destroying geysers and sometimes creating new ones. But these are changes according to nature's

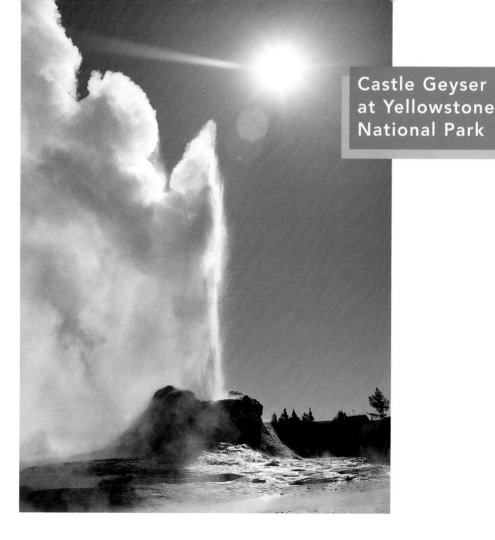

Castle Geyser
at Yellowstone
National Park

own plan. When people do
not damage their delicate
systems, geysers can go on
just as nature intended.

To Find Out More

Here are some additional resources to help you learn more about geysers:

Books

Bryan, T. Scott. **Geysers: What They Are and How They Work.** Roberts Rinehart, 1990.

Gallant, Roy A. **Geysers: When Earth Roars.** Franklin Watts, 1997.

Knapp, Patty. G**etting to Know Yellowstone National Park.** M. I. Adventure Publications, 1997.

Owens, Andy. **Geysers.** Heinemann Library, 2000.

Petersen, David. **Yellowstone National Park** (True Books). Children's Press, 1992.

Organizations and Online Sites

About Geysers
http://www2.wku.edu/www/ geoweb/geyser/about2.html

Learn what geysers are, why there are so rare, and how they work. Includes a map of areas of the world in which geysers are located.

Geysers and the Earth's Plumbing Systems
http://www.umich.edu/ ~gs265/geysers.html

A good explanation of the conditions necessary for geysers to form.

Geyser Observation and Study Association
P.O. Box 2852
Apple Valley, CA 92370

This organization provides current, accurate information about geysers and publishes a bimonthly newsletter about geysers.

Geyser Riser Homepage
http://creator.ns.msu.edu/ rise/group4/

General information about and photos of geysers.

Yellowstone National Park
http://www.yellowstonepark. com/

Yellowstone National Park is the site of more than half the world's geysers. Its website allows you to see Old Faithful erupt—a WebCam sends a new real-time photo of Old Faithful approximately every 35 seconds.

Important Words

eruption ejection of water from a geyser

fumarole vent in a geyser field that gives off steam and other gases because very little groundwater is present

geothermal energy energy tapped from hot water or steam in a volcanic region; the water is heated by molten rock deposits below Earth's surface

geyser hot spring that periodically throws hot water and steam into the air

geyserite brittle mineral deposit that forms around a hot spring

hot spring naturally occurring pool of water heated by geothermal energy

mud pot hot spring filled with boiling mud

spring opening at the Earth's surface that discharges water from underground sources

46

Index

Meet the Author

Larry Dane Brimner is an award-winning author of numerous books for young people. He has written many books for Children's Press, including a series of books about the planets. When he isn't visiting schools all across the United States to talk about the writing process with children and teachers, he lives in southern California.